LET'S TALK
PAIN & HEALING

ASHLEY R. MOORE, M.S.

Copyright © 2018 by Ashley R. Moore

All rights reserved. No part of this publication may be reproduced, distributed, or transmitted in any form or by any means, including photocopying, recording, or other electronic or mechanical methods, without the prior written permission of the publisher, except in the case of brief quotations embodied in critical reviews and certain other noncommercial uses permitted by copyright law.

ISBN: 978-1-945532-59-7

Printed in the United States of America

Published and Edited by:

Opportune Independent Publishing Co.
113 N. Live Oak Street
Houston, TX 77003
(832) 263-1700
www.opportunepublishing.com

Books may be purchased in large quantity and/or special sales by contacting mcgeea4676@gmail.com.

Dedication

This book is dedicated to my family. They have always inspired me to keep pushing and keep God first. My father was a great man of faith with encouraging words to say, and my mother challenged me daily. For that I am eternally grateful. I also dedicate this book to my loving husband, Brandon Moore. He has been my rock and my biggest supporter through school and my professional career.

Preface

This book relays experiences from different people with similar backgrounds. As a therapist, I have provided several mental health services including individual, family, and group therapy. These stories have been restructured for the purpose of this book and to maintain confidentiality. Please note: The characters in this book are fictional with real-life experiences.

TABLE OF CONTENTS

Chapter 1 5

Chapter 2 11

Chapter 3 15

Chapter 4 23

Chapter 5 27

Chapter 6 31

Chapter 7 35

Introduction

I have always been told everyone has a story. Well, here's mine. My name is Jennifer. I was born into what some may consider a large family. I have four brothers and one sister. I only have a relationship with one of my siblings. Her name is Anna. One would think I had it all, but that's not my reality. I have reached my mental break. As you keep reading, you'll learn my struggles—the good, the bad, and the ugly. My circle of support has grown, but it hasn't always been that way. I've struggled with depression and severe mood changes. Through it all, my story conveys my strength, and what I have learned will inspire you.

CHAPTER ONE

"Relationships"

We have learned in our early years how valuable relationships are. Having a sense of connectedness is a way of life. However, what do you do when you don't know what healthy relationships look like? Having a sense of connectedness was not something I've always shared. My life, my struggles, my pain damaged my ability to form bonds even with those closest to me.

I was born into what some may consider a large family. I am the youngest amongst my siblings, and I can admit, I required a lot of attention. I do not remember a lot of good things from my childhood. I can only recall the moments that have affected me the most. One of the most memorable stories told to me was when I was seven years old. This is the story that started it all, I guess. It started when I was still baking in the oven (my mother's womb, that is). My mom learned she was pregnant with me and she expressed how much she did not want me. Therefore, she decided to take medications in hopes to terminate the pregnancy herself. Clearly, that did not work because I'm here alive and well. But, can you imagine how something like that could damage a child? I thought no one wanted me, especially not my mother. We always argued, and I've always felt like she favored my sister. I built resentment toward both, Anna and my mother. Trust is something earned, and I didn't trust either one of them. My desire to have a relationship with either of them was non-existent. Unfortunately, I had to continue to stick around.

As sisters, Anna and I often fought physically. You would think it was normal. What siblings do you know who don't fight or argue? But in my case, it was way more than it should be; I believed she hated me. But why? When I was younger, I wasn't a fighter. I especially didn't want to go round-for-round with my sister. For every fight we had, I sat and wondered more and more what did I do to her that was so wrong. With the exception of being born, I couldn't figure out why she hated me so much.

As you could imagine, I often contemplated thoughts of suicide. I needed to escape. I remember being alone, thinking to myself, and wanting to escape. So, one of those days came when I had taken all I could take. My solution was to overdose on prescription medications. Like my mother, I wasn't successful either. Once found, I was taken to a hospital for treatment and later had to undergo an evaluation. A person can only take so much turmoil; I was at a point where I cried all the time and had no sense of purpose in life.

I never felt like I belonged at home with my family. No one should have to try to fit in at home; it should be automatic with your family. Instead, I often wondered where I would find the love I longed for. Feeling liked or loved was foreign to me; I was bullied at home and at school. I was an easy target for most, I guess. As one could imagine, it was difficult to find my voice, let alone my place in the world. It wasn't fair! I wanted to wake up from this nightmare.

The one person that was sure to bring light to my life was my father. He worked two jobs, so I wasn't always able to spend a lot of time with him. However, the times I did were nothing short of amazing. I was like a kid in a candy store. He took me fishing, talked to me about the Bible, and made sure all my basic needs were met. It was like night and day between my parents; I couldn't understand how he could be with someone like her. I guess opposites really do attract. There was one thing I knew for sure; I was daddy's little girl. As great as those times were, every child longs for love from their mother. It's usually unsaid or such a natural thing it doesn't have to be mentioned, but I was growing up with a void in my heart and didn't know how to fill it. And clearly, she had no intention to do so.

It's no shock that my mother physically, verbally, and emotionally abused me. It was heartbreaking, humiliating, and embarrassing. I've always been around girls my age who talked in the sense of their mother's being their best friend. I didn't have that experience. She burned me with irons, broke leather belts while beating me, and called me names that no child should ever be called. There were times that my name was seemingly changed to words like "bitch," "dumb," "stupid," "ugly," and sometimes "fat."

You would think my mother just hated kids or her children in particular. But, no, it was just me she hated. My sister, Anna, never seemed to do anything wrong in the eyes of my mother, although, she was the most disrespectful to her. Why me, and not her? Anna was popular in school, and I resented her for that too. She had many friends, played basketball, was on the homecoming court, and was a dancer. It was easier for her to accomplish so much in school because she had more support. I was never able to do anything unless my dad took me. And because of his busy work schedule, there weren't many opportunities. I tried to live in Anna's shadow, but I couldn't. I had no athletic capabilities, and I didn't feel pretty. So, I simply stayed a shadow.

Eventually, I stopped trying and became withdrawn with no desire to develop relationships with anyone. What was the point?

To make matters worse, I couldn't keep the abuse to myself. I wanted my younger cousin to feel that same pain. I would sometimes fight her because I knew she wouldn't fight back, and I threatened to hurt her more if she told on me. I was contributing to the cycle of abuse; they would hurt me, and I would hurt her. By this time, I was only ten years old. How was it possible that my life was so terrible that I inflicted the same pain onto those who were like me? She was harmless. It had gotten to the point to where I knew this pain had to come to an end. I had the perfect plan to get rid of it. Well, at least I thought so.

CHAPTER TWO

"The Betrayal"

By the age of 12, my father finally decided to leave my mother, and he took me with him. In my eyes, this was just the beginning of a great life; I thought the extended nightmare had finally ended. Little did I know, it was just the beginning. My father and my mother eventually got back together. It was very confusing and added to the drama that was already occurring between us. However, this time around she was cheating on him. I knew because she would often take me with her to betray my father. Not that she cared, but I would cry and threaten to tell my father in hopes that she would stop. But the betrayal carried on for years. When I would threaten to tell, she would beat the hell out of me and even threaten to kill me.

My father meant everything to me. How could I keep this from him? How could I risk my safety at home? For years to come, I did not say anything about her infidelity. It was like a knife tearing into my heart every time I was forced to witness her cheating. I felt like I was betraying the one person in my life whom I felt cared about me. What was a young girl to do?

As I grew older, I knew if I didn't begin to have a voice, I would never find my strength. So I started to find my inner strength. I chose to speak positivity into my life. Daily quotes, reading the bible, ongoing prayers, and affirmations. One day, I decided to sit down and tell my father everything she had been doing to me, and I even told him about my mother's infidelity. To say the least, I didn't get the reaction I anticipated. I was hoping we'd be on the first thing smoking.

But, he didn't leave her. Instead, he chose to honor his vows. Their relationship became very estranged. They began sleeping in separate bedrooms. I noticed my father stopped wearing his ring and was talking less and less. He prayed a lot more than normal, and he began to talk with me about the power of forgiveness. Although I understood what he meant, how could I forgive someone who hurt me so badly over and over? Someone who was supposed to love me, but didn't.

But life kept going on in the meantime.

By my high school years, I began to find myself more and more. However, I still had some issues developing and maintaining some friendships. It's true that children learn behaviors from their parents. I had no clue what type of friends I wanted or needed, nor did I know how to be a friend to others. People would tell me secrets, and I would spread the gossip all around school. When it did come back to me, I felt helpless. The bullying continued. I was so used to not defending myself that I couldn't.

I did get a lot of attention from the boys, but with the boys came the drama. So, I dated guys behind my parents back. I lied at home so that I could see them.

When I became old enough, I started working. My dad eventually gave in and bought me a car. It was one of the best things that could've happened to me. I lied about my work schedule so that I could get out of the house as much as possible. My home life was consistently going in circles; I felt trapped with no escape route.

It was time. I had to find myself and learn who I was, and not the names I was called. At the age of 16, I met a guy who I began dating.

It's interesting how we met. I went to a drive-in to get some food, and as I was leaving, I backed up and almost hit a guy with my car. He walked up to my car. I apologized immediately and asked him if he was okay. He told me he came to curse me out but was captured by my beauty. So, he decided to talk to me instead. We talked for a few minutes and exchanged numbers. Little did I know, my world would soon turn upside down even more within the blink of an eye. All because of this one guy!

CHAPTER THREE

"The Abuse"

Now, I have a boyfriend named Bash. Things between us started off pretty good. He was sweet and considerate in the beginning; however, he was very protective. Since I had never experienced anything like that before outside of my father, it was refreshing. I felt like someone, other than my father, finally loved me. Bash had a bit of a mean streak, but that's one of the things I admired about him.

So, one day on break at work, we were talking on the phone. He heard a coworker say some inappropriate things to me, and the next thing I knew, he was walking through the doors of my job. At first glimpse, I was under the impression that I was getting a surprise. That's exactly what I got. He ran into the back kitchen, punched my coworker, and ran off. I was terrified I would lose my job but appreciative that he wouldn't let anyone disrespect me.

A few weeks passed, and his mother called me frantically. All I could hear was screaming in the background. She told me he was upset and the only way he would calm down was if he were to talk to me.

I decided to visit him the day after his rant, and things were going well. He seemed to have calmed down completely. That is until I received a phone call and didn't answer my cell phone. He quickly became enraged. He locked me in his room, pushed me down, choked me, and threatened to kill me. This was too much of a reminder of my home life. I cried and pleaded with him. All he could say to me was how crazy he was over me, and he didn't want to lose me. When he finally let me go, I left in tears heading home. He called and apologized. And so easily, I accepted his apology. After all, pain and being treated badly was all I knew. My mother abused me, and she was supposed to love me, so I felt Bash loved me too. I replaced his abusive behavior with love in my head. I had no way of knowing his behavior was not the appropriate expression of love.

Fast forward.

It's now time for graduation. Bash came to my graduation, and we hung out a few times before I left for college.

He once asked me to meet him at a local convenience store to talk. When he pulled up, he drove his car straight into my brand new car. He jumped in my car and made me drive around the city. He was punching me for no reason while I was driving. Afraid to continue, I tried to pull over and put him out. He grabbed my steering wheel and said, "I'll make you hit a brick wall if you pull over." What do you think I did? I kept driving, of course.

On another occasion, I visited him at his relative's house, and we talked about his anger. That went terribly wrong!

This man had completely changed me, and not in a good way. I began to turn on the one person I loved so much in this world. I started to turn on my dad. You see, my dad was trying to teach me better, and I refused to listen. I kept seeing this guy despite what my father thought or said. He loved me. Right?

Bash had thrown televisions at me, punched me, and abused me in all forms. But because I loved him, I hid those bruises with makeup. He had kicked me repeatedly in my stomach, yet was always emotional and apologized.

One day, he shared with me his feelings about his absent father. He was a broken young boy, and all I wanted to do was help him. But how? I was broken too. I felt sorry for him, so I stayed in this relationship for a few years. I took the abuse and even made excuses for him.

Eventually, I went off to college and met new people. I started putting some distance between us, have fun and go out with "friends." I have to admit, I met some great people in college. I became really close to some guys I met, and they treated me like their little sister. They protected me and made sure I had everything I needed; they looked out for me.

Bash wasn't having it. He would drive three hours to come to my college and attack me. One night, he choked me, and a neighbor called one of the guys whom I considered to be a brother. Once my "brother" arrived, they got into a physical altercation.

Even then, did I leave him? No, I stayed. I knew he needed help. He agreed to go to a psychiatrist. It was exactly what he needed. He was diagnosed and given medication to help him control himself.

After that, he was doing really well, and we were making progress in our relationship. When he came to visit me, and for the first time after seeking help, I didn't fear him.

We were taking a nice drive, and all of a sudden, he felt himself become angry. Instead of taking his meds, he poured them out of the window. I remember thinking, "I have to get away from him," but I couldn't. He pulled a gun out and threatened to kill me because he heard I had been going out with friends and partying and he disapproved. When things did not go his way, he would lose it.

To escape, I had to play into his delusion. I admitted I was wrong and I could make things better. I deleted all of my contacts from my phone and ignored any phone calls. I told him he was right and I loved him and never wanted to hurt him. This was a switch as I would normally argue and fight—It worked; his behaviors and reactions were unpredictable, so my responses had to be too.

I was tired of being broken. It was up to me to learn my worth. I decided to call it quits. He convinced me to meet him in an open parking lot, and I did. I told him we were over and I gave back the necklace he had given me. He took my head and slammed it into the steering wheel of my car.

As I screamed, he got out and fled. I was headed back to school, and he called me repeatedly. I refused to answer the phone.

Besides, I had been talking to a guy I met while at college. He was the complete opposite of Bash; he didn't have a mean streak. He was so sweet but lacked the ability to commit to any type of relationship. Considering I was fresh out of a relationship, I saw no harm in it. This time, I was finding my happy place. That is until I learned about the many other women he was talking to.

I thought to myself, "You guys are just having fun, it's not exclusive." I didn't know I was experiencing another form of abuse. I decided to take a deep look in the mirror. If all these bad things are happening to me, maybe it's not them. It's me. I left that guy alone and started focusing on myself.

I took an art class, and there was this athlete who always noticed when I was absent. He appeared to be a nice guy, but my experience had taught me it never led to anything good, so I ignored him. I gave him the wrong number a few times, and so on.

My junior year rolled around, and he was still trying to court me. I gave it a try. It was the best decision I could've ever made. He was passionate, considerate, smart, and well-rounded, just an overall good guy. He was a good communicator, and I was just learning how to communicate in relationships and with people in general properly. The only way I knew how to communicate was through anger.

As time went by, he introduced me to his parents and everything was going well. He was slowly transforming me, and I'm not even sure he knew it. The relationship was heaven sent.

He graduated a year before me and left to go back home to Chicago. Of course, I pleaded for him to stay in Alabama with me. After a while, I began to learn a new side of him. He was becoming overbearing. He wanted to dictate where I could go, who I could go with, and tried to make me feel like I had no one in this world but him. When I tried to break up with him, he threatened to kill himself. I decided I wouldn't fall for that again. I told him I hope he wouldn't and wished him well.

A few weeks later, I called to check on him. Surprise, surprise—he was still alive. After a refreshing talk, we decided to be friends and work on ourselves individually in hopes that we would get back together eventually.

CHAPTER FOUR

"It Doesn't Come Easy"

A year had passed, and it was my turn to graduate from college. I realized then that we couldn't recover our relationship, so it was over. If I was going to find my peace, I had to focus on myself. So that's exactly what I did. I moved back home for a short period of time, but I knew I had to find a job and leave as soon as possible.

My mother would look at me as if she was disgusted and would often call me, "Bitch." Her anger was still just as strong for me, if not stronger. One night, she took a cast iron skillet off the stove and attempted to hit me across the head.

I learned at that point what fight or flight truly

meant. Let me explain. "Fight or flight" is a physiological response that happens when you perceive a threat to your survival or encounter a harmful event. At that moment, I knew I had to defend myself. I am not proud of fighting my mother, and I have prayed for forgiveness. But after that incident, I left and never turned back. I went back to school to get out of the house, and I eventually began to work.

Along came James; I met him at work. He was the cutest guy ever! He changed his schedule to reflect mine, and he was the just sweetest thing. We had fun together, my friends liked him, and he never tried to control me. We were just friends for a long time because I was still on the journey of finding myself and searching for my peace. And he respected that. I did not hide how broken I was from him. In fact, it was difficult for him to believe all the pain I'd been through.

He was so patient. After some time, when I felt like I was at peace, we decided to take our relationship to another level. He had small habits, but nothing that could affect me. However, I had to learn to take responsibility for my decisions. I had to decide if I wanted to take a detour or continue my journey of happiness. I chose my happiness.

James and I decided to be in a committed relationship where he showed me a love like I have never known before. I prayed that I would find a husband who was a true reflection of my father—someone who would cherish me, provide for me, and build with me. We would thrive together. And we did just that! After two years of dating, James asked me to marry him! It was the best day of my life. My dad gave his blessing, but of course, my mother didn't seem too happy. I shouldn't be surprised though, right? But I was.

Oddly enough, I went wedding dress shopping with my husband-to-be because I had no one else. I tried on a few dresses to get his opinion, but he didn't know which dress I had chosen, so it was all good! I worked with an aspiring wedding coordinator, so I hired her to help me plan my wedding. The entire experience was beautiful. It seemed like my life was taking a turn for the better. James and I vacationed all of the time, and we held each other accountable in our marriage. However, James didn't believe my mother was as bad as the picture I painted. Clearly, he was in for a rude awakening.

CHAPTER FIVE

"She Strikes Again"

One day, I received a phone call from my estranged sister, Anna. Her and my mother had a recent fight. The only time I get information from her is when they aren't speaking. She told me my mother was spreading disgusting lies about my father and I sleeping together. Nothing could be further from the truth. Is it a crime to be close to your father? Out of all the things she's ever done to me, this was the most hurtful. I felt my emotions spiraling out of control, and I didn't know how to contain them. My family had struck yet again!

My husband was so supportive during my time of weakness. It was at that point I decided to cut my mother off completely. This was the last straw for me. When my father and I spoke regarding this terrible rumor, although he was hurt, he guided me to the Bible, as usual. He told me I had to learn the power of forgiveness, that it's not for the other person; it was for me. I forgave her and decided to move on.

However, our relationship became quite exhausting. We were off and on again every other month. It was crazy. If she felt like talking, we would talk. If she didn't, then I wouldn't hear from her for weeks at a time. I was beginning to resent her. My husband couldn't understand how I could constantly allow her to hurt me over and over again. I didn't know how to explain it to him. This has been part of my life forever. This is a piece of the puzzle I can't seem to put in its rightful place. A piece of my life I couldn't escape from.

I don't know what it feels like to get a hug, be told "I love you," or have girl talks with my mother, not even my sister for that fact. I envied my peers for that. They had great relationships with their moms and referred to them as their best friend. Meanwhile, I'm always thinking, *my mother doesn't even like me*. If felt like the only time she would have anything to do with me was if she was able to get something out of me.

The following Christmas, she wasn't speaking to me again. I bought gifts for my immediate family and decided I wasn't going to leave her out. Little did I know, I would receive a big box at my doorstep. I thought it was a gift. Sure enough, it was, but it was the one I bought her. It had a message on the box in bold letters—"**I AM NOT YOUR MOTHER**."

Ouch!!!!!! What could I have done that was so bad she wanted to continue to tear me down? Was it even possible for her to tear me down even more? Yup, and that's exactly she did! Yet again, I allowed this to happen. This is my truth! I cried for hours and hours trying to figure out how to put my life back together. It was easy to erase the people who weren't related to me out of my life, but how did I erase the lady who gave birth to me? Is that even possible? I had to realize that all the trying in the world wouldn't make the people or things around me change. So, now what was I to do?

I had to pick up the pieces I did have to the puzzle and start putting them in their rightful place. I was hoping for the best but learned to prepare myself for the worst. I was preparing myself for the possibilities of upset when it came to my mom, which allowed me to feel less pain.

CHAPTER SIX

"Exchanging Old For New"

First, I had to acknowledge the things in my life that impacted me the most. I have an estranged relationship with my mother and sister. I even have other siblings I have no relationship with because I don't know them! I'm afraid I don't know how to love because I was never really shown the true meaning of it until I met my husband.

I have developed a very bad temper. I must admit, I am a walking time bomb! I have to make other people feel just as bad as I do, if not worse. I have no filter on ANYTHING! I tend to be physically aggressive as well.

How do I change that? I'm going to switch my old behaviors for new ones. For every angry or negative action, I will replace it with a calm a positive one. I am practicing meditation. I will find my safe place, put on the most relaxing music, sit in a comfortable position, and reflect on the words to the songs. My choice is always gospel music. It takes me to a place where I want to be good. I want to master being calm so I can respond in a more socially appropriate way. I know that I am enough, so meditation helps me center myself! I get to spend time with me and me only, no one else to depend on. Why? Because my happiness starts with me and no one else. Once you master your worth in knowing you are enough; you are strong; you can conquer anything! My mental and physical health was no longer under attack. I've learned to simply let go.

Other ways you can exchange old behaviors for new ones is to learn to fight fair. I often found myself lashing out at my husband. Thankfully he never reacted! In order to fight fair one must:

- Refrain from teasing others.
- Refrain from physical aggression.
- Avoid yelling.
- Don't interrupt when others are talking.
- Avoid attacking the other person's personality.

- Avoid calling one another names.
- Do not bring up the past.
- Don't try to get the last word.

Instead,
- Discuss one issue at a time.
- Communicate calmly and talk to one another, not at one another.
- Use "I feel" to state how you feel.
- Be willing to forgive, compromise, and negotiate.
- Take responsibility for your actions
- Focus on solutions
- Take the time you need to remain calm
- Listen, and don't just listen to respond! Truly listen!!!!!!

CHAPTER SEVEN

"Look For The Good"

Often times, when we get caught up in the negativity in our lives, that's all we tend to see. It's important to look for the good in people, including those who have hurt you. Stop focusing on the bad things you see and redirect your focus to look for the good in others that will contribute to your healing. This is one of the hardest things to do.

Regarding my mother, I could tell you all the wrong things she has done in my life, but that will not contribute to my healing. Therefore, I choose to see the qualities she possesses. Surprisingly, she can be very caring. She has a natural gift to be a caregiver, which is quite strange. Believe it or not, she is really good at it! She is willing to help if she can, and I believe deep down she has a soul and is capable of loving. Maybe she is broken and doesn't know how to love.

Set a goal to notice the good in others during some of your most trying moments. Keep a record of those times and make the decision to see the good instead of criticizing. This process is for your healing. You will learn to control your emotions in a healthier way. These techniques have transformed my life completely. These days, I smile a lot more and cry a lot less. I have acknowledged my past, my actions, and now I have started my journey to healing.

I am now a successful African American mentor dedicated to helping our youth who come from broken homes. I am helping them discover their healing. No matter your background, no matter who has broken you, it's never too late to put the pieces of the puzzle back together again.

I am happily married, growing a family of my own, and am excelling in my career. I have come too far to stop now. This is only the beginning, but there are greater things to come! I have taken you on a journey in hopes to inspire you. People view therapy as something bad, or only crazy participate in therapy. It is the complete opposite. It's healing and identification of self! Rejoice with truth, always protect, trust, and remain hopeful. Always persevere!

www.ingramcontent.com/pod-product-compliance
Lightning Source LLC
Chambersburg PA
CBHW071548080526
44588CB00011B/1827